- 3
- HOLE
- PRESS

Soho Rep. Special Edition 2019

First performance at Soho Rep., New York:
February 6, 2018.

ISBN: 978-0-9982763-4-2

**3 Hole Press** books are distributed by
Small Press Distribution and printed in the USA
by McNaughton & Gunn on recycled paper.

Design by Omnivore

**3 Hole Press**
Brooklyn NY
3holepress.org

# Is God Is

*Cast*

| | |
|---|---|
| RACINE | Dame-Jasmine Hughes |
| ANAIA | Alfie Fuller |
| SHE | Jessica Frances Dukes |
| CHUCK HALL | Michael Genet |
| RILEY | Anthony Cason |
| SCOTCH | Caleb Eberhardt |
| ANGIE | Nehassaiu deGannes |
| MAN | Teagle F. Bougere |

*Creative Team*

| | |
|---|---|
| PLAYWRIGHT | Aleshea Harris |
| DIRECTOR | Taibi Magar |
| SCENIC DESIGNER | Adam Rigg |
| COSTUME DESIGNER | Montana Levi Blanco |
| LIGHTING DESIGNER | Matthew Richards |
| SOUND DESIGNER | Jeremy Toussaint-Baptiste |
| FIGHT DIRECTOR | J. David Brimmer |
| HAIR AND WIG DESIGNER | Cookie Jordan |
| PROPS DESIGNER | Samantha Shoffner |
| | |
| PRODUCTION STAGE MANAGER | Danielle Teague-Daniels |
| ASSISTANT STAGE MANAGER | Genevieve Ortiz |

Funding for *Is God Is* is provided, in part, by the
Venturous Theater Fund of the Tides Foundation.


Soho Rep.'s return to Walker Street is made
possible with leadership support from:

The Tow Foundation
Dorothy Berwin
Barry Feirstein
Howard Gilman Foundation
James Gleick and Cynthia Crossen
Janice Lee and Stuart Shapiro
Jim and Laura Pizzo
Caryl Ratner
The Seth Sprague Educational and
    Charitable Foundation

The Soho Rep. 2017–2018 season is made possible with support from the following INNER CIRCLE members and all our generous donors.

**$50,000+**
Andrew W. Mellon Foundation, Barry Feirstein, Howard Gilman Foundation, James Gleick & Cynthia Crossen, Janice Lee & Stuart Shapiro, Jim & Laura Pizzo, Caryl Ratner, Shubert Foundation, The Tow Foundation, Venturous Theater Fund of the Tides Foundation, The Vilcek Foundation

**$25,000 – $49,999**
Dorothy Berwin, The Berwin-Lee Foundation, Fan Fox & Leslie R. Samuels Foundation, Frank Holozubiec, Victoria Meakin, National Endowment for the Arts, Tim Blake Nelson, New York City Department of Cultural Affairs, New York State Council on the Arts, Mace Rosenstein & Louise de la Fuente, The Seth Sprague Educational and Charitable Foundation, Harold & Mimi Steinberg Charitable Trust, Virginia B. Toulmin Foundation

**$10,000 – $24,999**
Jennifer Adler, Kashif Akhter, Jodi & Craig Balsam, Shepard Barbash & Vicki Ragan, Don & Maggie Buchwald, The Corner Foundation, Jon & Lou Dembrow, The Durst Organization, Alfred F. Hubay, Branden Jacobs-Jenkins, The Jerome Foundation, John Miller, MRC, Jody Falco & Jeffrey Steinman, The Dorothy Strelsin Foundation, Studio Usher, Diane C. Yu & Michael Delaney

## $5,000 – $9,999

Steven & Sheila Aresty Foundation, Axe-Houghton Foundation, Marc Baum, New York City Council Member Margaret Chin, Ed & Doris Cohen, Susan & Thomas Dunn, Leah Gardiner & Seth Gilliam, The John Golden Fund, Alexander Greenberg, John Isaacs, JMJ Family Fund, Judi & Douglas Krupp, Leon Levy Foundation, Lucille Lortel Foundation, Stephen & Carolyn McCandless, Zach & Alissa Miller, Ann & Richard Passen, Patrick Ravey, The Jerome Robbins Foundation, Joe Robertson, The Rudin Foundation, Inc., Jon & Nora Lee Sedmak, The Shepherd Foundation, Joanne & Daniel C. Smith, Starry Night Fund, The Still Point Fund, Lisa Van Curen, Frank Williams, anonymous

## $2,000 – $4,999

Alexandra Alger & Dan Chung, Roberta Balsam, The Barbara Bell Cumming Charitable Trust, Andrea Benzacar & Barbara F. Hughes, Ann Berman, Alan Bersin, Annie Chanler, Joan Cohen, Scott Delman, Todd Donovan, Jeanne Donovan Fisher, Laura Fontana, Ford Foundation, Britt-Louise Gilder, Sue & Jed Isaacs, Neil LaBute, Margie Becker-Lewin & John Lewin, The Magid Family Fund, Rona & Randolph M. Nelson Foundation, Madeleine Noveck, Tom Pastore, Bernadette & James Polsky, Linda Powell, Jonah Pregerson, The Richenthal Foundation, Judith O. Rubin, Joshua Shapiro & Heller B. Berman, Jonathan Marc Sherman & Alexandra Shiva, Muriel F. Siebert Foundation, Sarah Solomon, Marlene Swartz & Jerry Engelbach, TheaterMania, anonymous

*Donor list updated December 2017.*
*Every effort is made to keep it accurate and up-to-date.*

*This epic takes its cues from the ancient, the modern, the tragic, the Spaghetti Western, hip-hop and Afropunk.*

*This text also includes adventures in typography.*

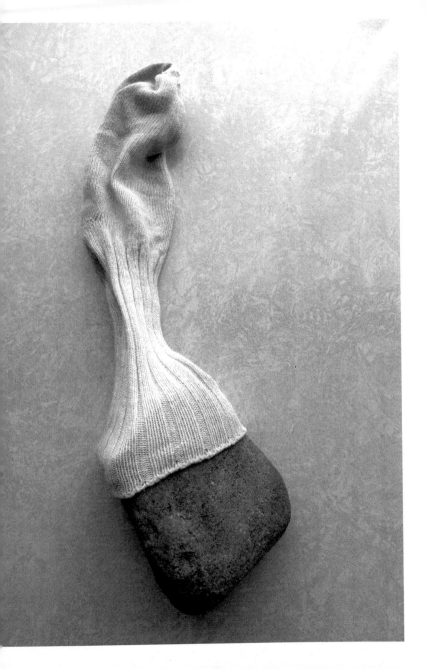

# IS
# GOD
# IS

**A Play by**
**Aleshea Harris**

**SPECIAL THANKS**

To Douglas Kearney, Brian Carbine,
Heather L. Jones and Mona Heinze
for taking the time to read and give feedback.

To Rachel Kauder Nalebuff for patience,
belief and a remarkable commitment to new work.

For Ma,
who holds the babies despite the burning.

# Introduction

What my mother was taught about the story of Cain and Abel, and what she believes, is that the "mark of Cain" is not only a curse but also the raced black body itself. She is eager to point out that the suffering of black people is Biblical prophesy, immutable damnation. This flawed exegesis is not her own, of course, but instead on loan from the minister at her church who taught Bible study many years ago. It's heavy to me that black people themselves can find solace in this rendition of human history in which God, rather than humans of their own accord, with their own agency, created black misery. It makes the history and condition of black life not merely a result of human barbarism, but analogous to the legend of the Wandering Jew, endlessly cursed with displacement until the Second Coming. A locked door. What's one to do?

Certainly, *Is God Is* is a twist on the Biblical story of two brothers—one good, one murderous. However allegorical Harris's play might be, it does not purport to put forth any prophesy related to the "curse" of the raced body. Instead, we are made acutely aware of the universal struggle within and against that which looks a lot like evil. This struggle is not exceptional, but is a condition of human life. A complicated stickiness inside each of us.

Our cultural insistence on the presumption of the singular self is disrupted in *Is God Is* by irredeemable violence. Violence, like other traumas, fragments the self and removes the ground from below us. We are left floating and piecemeal in the wake of violence. Before the script even begins, our protagonists' bodies are set on fire. Out of flames, the mutant twins Racine and Anaia, fractured by the gap between the burned body and the recognizable self, narrate their movements as if from the outside looking in. Racine says, "Racine is the rough one who still got some pretty to her." The characters function both as narrator and subject, standing inside the body and outside of it, begging the question of whether the condition of dual consciousness is a condition of black human existence a la W.E.B. DuBois's oft-cited claim. Harris seems to want tie a tether between the human history of brutality on the planet and the raced body itself. We are left to wonder whether the black body, in particular, is always already a site of violence, and thus a split self from the moment it takes its first breath.

I cannot help but think, as well, of Adrienne Kennedy's phenomenal one-act play, *Funnyhouse of a Negro*, which premiered off Broadway in 1964. In it, the protagonist Sarah, who struggles with her biraciality, is split into several selves—so much so that the other characters are each "one of herselves." Sarah courts her European ancestry and is haunted by her African ancestry, creating a fissure of insistence that catalyzes a kind of madness. The violence of the attack on the twins and their mother in Harris's play catapults a similar madhouse of splintered identity.

\* \* \*

A cross of protection hangs dumbly on my mother's bedroom door.

To make my contempt parenthetical feels safer.

Crevice that countenances the actual.

Special conditions arise when placing the head in the lion's mouth.

Are we ever safe?

Unanswerable questions abound. Comfort is fiction. To be comfortable to is to cut off a portion of experience and live in bracketed space. It requires delusion.

\* \* \*

What is the form in which something wants to be said? Why the devotion to rigid boundaries of genre? Aleshea Harris's *Is God Is* defies genre categories and reaches toward a productive oblivion. This oblivion is evident in the texture of the surreal narrative, itself an incarnation of the brutalizations of black women's bodies. No one is redeemed in Harris's narrative. No one is simply "good" while another simply "evil." To the contrary, and unlike the dichotomous Cain and Abel, the brutal spreads throughout Harris's genre-defying play like a chemical weapon, poisoning everything in its path. No easy answers. No fictional safeties.

What Harris's work undertakes instead of fictional safeties and causalities are the problems of utterance, transgressions, and violence as a gendered category writ large into cultural space. There will be a moment when reading, when you will root for our twins, when you will be on their side as they seek what appears initially to be a redemptive justice; but this moment will disintegrate and splinter into the gasping air. Typography indicates these glaring elisions, foregrounding instead registers of speech or feelings that are not usually visible in the genre itself but are imposed in the interpretation or the staging. It is here that we feel relief, in that formal exploration that usurps our ordinary ideas about what a play does and what kinds of knowledge discoveries it can make. Aleshea Harris's *Is God Is* is a rigorous work, a new wave of blaxploitation that unearths our deepest fears about humanity and who we think we are in relation to ourselves and the divine.

—*Dawn Lundy Martin*
  *Marfa, Texas*

# Characters

**RACINE** African-American. A woman of twenty-one years. Identical twin sister to ANAIA. Has burn scars on her arms, back and neck but a face of considerable beauty.

**ANAIA** Has burn scars on her arms, face and neck. Hard to look at. Wears a wig.

**SHE** African-American. Mother to RACINE and ANAIA. Has burn scars over her entire body.

**CHUCK HALL** African-American. A lawyer. Middle-aged.

**RILEY** African-American. A boy of sixteen.

**SCOTCH** African-American. A boy of sixteen.

**ANGIE** African-American. Mother to RILEY and SCOTCH.

**MAN** African-American. A father.

# Scenes

A LETTER

BEFORE GOD

GOING WEST

THE WEAPON

IN THE VALLEY

UP TO THE HILLS

THE HOUSE ON THE HILL

IN THE ROAD

TWINS & TWINS

DRESSING

THE TEASE

ALL FALL DOWN

SHOWDOWN

TWIN?

AGAIN BEFORE GOD

# *A Letter*

(*A blazing inferno. Out of the fire step ANAIA and RACINE.*

*A studio apartment in the Northeast.*

*ANAIA rubs the scars on RACINE's back with ice as the fire subsides.*)

**RACINE & ANAIA**
Twins.

**RACINE**
Burnin
Them burnin twins
at home in their apartment
in the Northeast
New York or Hampshire
or Jersey

**ANAIA**
or
Somethin like that
Somewhere that don't feel right

**RACINE & ANAIA**
Twins

**RACINE**
Racine is the rough one who still got some pretty to her. She only got the scars on her back and a bit creeping up the rear of her neck. You can barely see 'em.

**ANAIA**

Anaia wasn't so lucky. Face look like it melted
and then froze. Mostly people don't let their eyes
meet hers.

**RACINE**

'Cine used the handle of a rake to shut Tommy
Danson up in the seventh grade when he called
'Naia a bad name. Thas the kinda roughness she got.

**ANAIA**

'Naia is trapped in a prison of sweetness. Girl so
ugly don't get to be mean.

**RACINE**

'Cine does though. She got both their mean.

(*to ANAIA*) Got somethin today.

**ANAIA**

'Naia's too tired for this.
She work in a warehouse packing cold things into
boxes all day.
She's too tired for this—

**RACINE**

In the mail. Got somethin. News.

**ANAIA**

'Naia keep her head down out of habit.
O, yeah? I got news, too.

**RACINE**

This big, tho.
Got a letter with some news in it. Big news.

**ANAIA**

Letter from who?

**RACINE**
From
Mama.

**ANAIA**
From who?

**RACINE**
From Mama.

**ANAIA**
Who Mama?

**RACINE**
Our Mama.

**ANAIA**
We got a mama?

**RACINE**
We do.

**ANAIA**
Too tired for this
         I thought she was dead.

**RACINE**
Well. She ain't.

**ANAIA**
I thought she was dead in a fire. Same fire that put these marks on us.

**RACINE**
Well, she ain't.

**ANAIA**
Well, what she want? Where she been?

**RACINE**
You gettin all worked up. Switch.

(*ANAIA sits. RACINE rubs ice on ANAIA's scars.*)

She wanna see us. She been in a place. A place for sick people who old.

**ANAIA**
Uh old folks' home?

**RACINE**
I think so.

(*Takes an envelope from her pocket. Reads.*)

"Folsom Rest Home for the Weary.
2115 Pluckum Drive
Oscarville, MS/AL/FL/TX/TN/AR/KY
Dirty South 39582313650849"

**ANAIA**
Thas where she at?

**RACINE**
Eyup.

**ANAIA**
Damn.          Thas where she been at?

**RACINE**
Seem like it.

**ANAIA**
Damn.

**RACINE**
Hey Twin.

**ANAIA**
Yeah?

**RACINE**
Seem like we got to go to where she at.

**ANAIA**
Go?

**RACINE**
Yeah.

**ANAIA**
But we don't know her and she don't know us.

**RACINE**
She know our names and she knew how to find us. We got to go see her.

**ANAIA**
Well, why she ain't come see us in all these years? Ask about us?

**RACINE**
Only one way to find out. Les go.

**ANAIA**
Now?

**RACINE**
Eyup. Right now 'cause she' finna go.

**ANAIA**
Where she finna go?

**RACINE**
Die.

**ANAIA**
Die?

**RACINE**
Eyup. Says so in the letter.

**ANAIA**
Damn, 'Cine.

**RACINE**
I know it.

**ANAIA**
She only wrote to you? She ain't write me?

**RACINE**
Ain't but my name on the envelope, but she talk about you.

**ANAIA**
Why she ain't write me?

**RACINE**
Maybe 'cause she knew you'd be all emotional.

**ANAIA**
Me?

**RACINE**
Yeah, you. Even though she ain't been around us she prolly got uh intuition about it. Mamas be knowin bout stuff like that. She can prolly sense how you be gettin all emotional, all sad-sack-y—

**ANAIA**
I don't be.

**RACINE**
You do.

**ANAIA**
Don't.

**RACINE**
Do. You cried about that kitten we couldn't get outta the engine. The one that died?

**ANAIA**
It died 'cause you wasn't patient enough to coax it out.

**RACINE**
Had to get to work. You cried. 'Member?
All emotional.

**ANAIA**
...chyeahhhhhh I guess thas true. I do be all emotional sometimes—

**RACINE**
Like a lil punk.

**ANAIA**
Yeah, yeah, ha ha—

**RACINE**
Like a lil bish

**ANAIA**
Now you takin it too far.

**RACINE**
I'm playin.

**ANAIA**
I got stuff to do, though. I gotta meet up with Ellis and tell him about something—

**RACINE**
Ellis who?

                    O. him.

**ANAIA**
Yeah. We sposed to meet up.

**RACINE**
'Cine sigh and roll her eyes like,
          "Here we go again
             bout that man she met online."

*(to ANAIA)* What you gotta meet up with him for?

**ANAIA**
We sposed to meet up and talk about    the future.

**RACINE**
'Cine bite her tongue.

*(to ANAIA)* Mhmm.
Switch.

*(They switch positions and ANAIA is now applying ice to RACINE's scars.)*

You love him?

**ANAIA**
No. But I don't want him to leave.

**RACINE**
Then do what you gotta do to keep him.

**ANAIA**
He don't like me to look at him when we doin it.

**RACINE**
So don't look at him. Put your pride away.
Some of us don't get to have pride.

**ANAIA**
True.

**RACINE**
So, let him get it from behind. If you look at him
you might start to catch feelins.

**ANAIA**
True, true.

**RACINE**
And we ain't got time for bein weak with feelins
for no man, 'Naia.
We got things to do.
She waitin on us.

**ANAIA**
She finna go, huh?
Go die, huh?

**RACINE**
Eyup. She finna go so we gotta go.

**ANAIA**

          damn.

**RACINE**
I
know.

**ANAIA**
W e l l
I guess I'll catch him later—

**RACINE**
Thas right. You can catch ol' dude later.
We need to look good since this kinda like
our first and last time seein her, don't you think?
I'm finna dress up. I'm wearin lipstick and all.

**NAIA**
Ima put me on some too.

**RACINE**
And a dress.

**ANAIA**
You don't never wear dresses. You be on that
"boho, I'm so pretty I ain't gotta try" shit.

**RACINE**
Yeah, but this is        Mama
                         we talkin 'bout.

**ANAIA**
I feel ya.

(*They are both getting pretty-fied.*)

That lipstick real red.

**RACINE**
Eyup.

**ANAIA**
Like how it feel to know she comin and goin.

**ANAIA & RACINE**
You look good. Thanks.
Think she'll like it?
Yeah. Yeah. Yeah.

\* \* \*

# *Before God*

(*The TWINS stand before an immense door.*)

**RACINE**
We in it. This is it. Folsom Rest Home for the Weary.
2115 Pluckum Drive
Oscarville, MS/AL/FL/TX/TN/AR/KY
Dirty South 39582313650849
Room 416B
And a sign with our names on it.
She musta did that so we'd know
we was in the right place.

**ANAIA**
My name ain't spelt right.

**RACINE**
O, come on, 'Naia.

**ANAIA**
You think she still alive?

**RACINE**
Only one way to find out.

**ANAIA**
My mascara runnin?

**RACINE**
A little.

**ANAIA**
Iss hot.

**RACINE**
Yeah. Dirty South stay hot.

**ANAIA**
You ready?

**RACINE**
To see God?

**ANAIA**
God?

**RACINE**
Well, she made us, didn't she?

**ANAIA**
You gon' get struck down.

**SHE**
A n a i a?    R a c i n e?

(*They look at one another.*)

That y'all?

**ANAIA**
You go on in.

**RACINE**
You first.

**SHE**
I can f e e l y'all out there.

**ANAIA**
First born is the first one in.

**RACINE**
Thas stupid.

**SHE**

you're wastin　　　　you're wastin

　　　　　　　　　　time.

(*SHE is wheezing. SHE lies on her deathbed. SHE huffs, coughs and struggles to breathe. Her voice comes out in hoarse rasps.*)

I'm

so glad

you

could make it.

Had　　　the nurse
　　put the sign out by my door
　　　　　　a sign with your names on it

see it?

**RACINE**

Yes, mama.
We. We
We really liked that sign.
We seen it.

**ANAIA**

　　　　　　　　　　　　My name ain't spelt right.

**SHE**

Good. Lemme look at y'all.

(*They step closer.*)

Okay. I see.
Anaia and Racine.
Used to put y'all in opposite clothes so I could tell you apart.

Anaia you was always in tropical colors and
Racine I had you in pastels. No matchy-matchy
for my girls.

**RACINE**
Thas nice. Now I like tropical and 'Naia like
pastels.

**ANAIA**
Thas a lie.

**RACINE**
Shut up.
    So. How you been?

**SHE** (*laughs*)
O, you know.
            Dyin.

**RACINE**
Yeah, yeah. I see you got them tubes in you.
We came soon as we could. Had to take off work
but we here.
I work at a daycare and 'Naia work in a warehouse.
She got a boyfriend.

**ANAIA**
thas a lie

**SHE**
She got something else, too.

**RACINE**
Ma'am?

**SHE**
Nothin. She quiet.

**ANAIA**

       hi mama.

**SHE**

I ain't wrote you, 'Naia
'cause you be gettin all emotional. Been that way
since you was little. I know.
I ain't wanna upset you.

**ANAIA**

I
I know.
       Thank you.

**SHE**

My girls.

**RACINE**

Yeah.

**SHE**

My baby girls.

**RACINE**

Eyup. Thas us.

**SHE**

Y'all are lookin at The Last Days
I keep tellin myself,
      "Ruby, this might be your last Thursday
         your last time wakin up in this bed
         your last time thinkin iss your last time"

(*SHE laughs. TWINS join, nervously.*)

Y'all done got so big.

**ANAIA**

Yeah. Been eighteen years.

**SHE**
Eyup.

**ANAIA**
We thought you was dead.

**SHE**
Thas what I wanted y'all to think.
             Who want
             a mama
                  with a body
                  like uh
                  a l l i g a t o r ?

**ANAIA**
Why
why you got a body like uh alligator?

**SHE**
'Causa what he did.

**ANAIA**
He who?

**SHE**
They ain't told y'all.

**RACINE**
Naw, they just said you was dead.

**ANAIA**
So we a little confused 'cause you alive but you ain't write us
or nothin.

**RACINE**
But we ain't really worried about all that—

**ANAIA**

Eighteen years. Been eighteen years.

(*An awkward pause.*)

**SHE**

Was that
      an awkward pause?

(*SHE laughs. RACINE joins, nervously.*)

All you know is it was a fire and your mama was
gone, huh?

| **RACINE** | **ANAIA** |
|---|---|
| Thas pretty much | Yeah. |
| what we been told. | |

**SHE**

      Well
      i'm 'on tell you
      there's more.

Had it all sealt up
so you could walk without shame
but iss more and you need to know it
so you understand your mama ain't just
              up and leave you
          iss more to it than that

**ANAIA**

What more?

**SHE**

I'll tell you            It was a regular day.
I had took y'all to daycare
and went to work. Regular day.
Got off work, got y'all and came home,
a baby in each arm. Y'all was three.

We get home and I put y'all in the kitchen
at the table with some apple slices—a snack
while I made dinner.
I had just chopped the onions at the counter
          I'll never forget it
   just chopped the onions when I heard the
window in the bathroom shut.

*(A kind of flashback. SHE retreats into the past,
hearing the window, suspicious.)*

Hello?
The T.V. Cartoons—loud

Hello?

The curtains in the kitchen—breathin.
The onion on the cutting board—waitin.
I rinse my hands and wipe 'em on my dress,
iss an old dress.

Hello? I pat your baby-heads, go down the hall
Maybe just a branch against the window
Hello?
Only, ain't no trees near our windows
Hello?
Down the hall. Bathroom door wide open.
Dark in there.
The mirror showing my scared silhouette.
Nothin in here but a bone-tired woman.

*(SHE laughs)*

My hand goes to the light switch
just to be, just to be sure, you know?
Can't be too careful
He said he was gon come back, so
Just to be sure
And the green light flashes on
and issa hand on the shower curtain
O god

The fear like an ax to the middle of my chest
O no
His hand, he pull the curtain aside
kinda sweet-like and
it reminds me of why I fell in love with him
he do got a tender side
he pull the curtain aside and just stands there

No smile or nothin. No frown, neither.
Face as plain as a slice of wheat bread.

"Hey"

He says, like we on the street or somethin
like he ain't just break into my bathroom
like it wasn't no restraining order
I couldn't even scream or nothin

                    Just

"Hey. You back."

A nod.
My mouth is twitching and my guts is on fire

"The kids are in the kitchen. I was just making
dinner—"

And iss like a train runs into my throat
He grips                    hard.
That same plain face right up next to mine,
        barely sweatin
and even lookin at me in a tender way
I can hear what sounds like a lullaby just before
everything turns dark.

(*Sound of a liquid being poured and MAN whistling.*)

*Is God Is*

When I come to I smell it.
Liquor. Issa sickly sweet smell.
Soaked in it.
Good thing this dress is old
It wouldn't never come out.

And he's whistling like a little bird while he do it.
His boots step all in it. He's whistling and pouring
Not rushing, just easy. He's gonna kill me easy.
Then the boots are still. Here go. Here go.
I close my eyes

                              but nothin happens.
A full minute passes—all I hear is my breath
and you two in the kitchen
giggling like how babies giggle
like they got the sun in they mouth
              ya know?

And the boots move tward y'all in the kitchen
And I can't talk 'cause he took the wind outta
my mouth
but in my throat is a rattle like:

                    "Don't you fucking touch
                         my babies!!!"

But he already bringin y'all.
    'Cine, I think he was holding you.
    'Naia, you was walking. One of y'all was sayin
"daddy where you been?" And he sayin
"on the Moon"
                         "the mooooon?"
"Yup. With the aliens."
And by now y'all in the bathroom standing over me.
And 'Cine, you wasn't scared. You said to him
"Daddy...whasss wrong with Mommy? What she
on the ground for?"

And he said, "Mommy's sleepy and she want
us to wake her up. You gonna help me wake
her up, Anaia?"
And 'Naia, you was always the emotional one, you
could tell somethin was off and you was scared.
You say,

"I    I   wanna   I wanna go back and watch
Scooby Doo."
"Just a minute. Let's wake Mommy up."

"How?"

"Like this."

(*A sound like a thousand matches being struck
simultaneously.*)

And 'Naia went to whining.
                "daddy        i  don't like this."
And then he musta dropped that little bit of fire
on me 'cause it was all on me gettin bigger,
that quick
eatin through me 'til my brain was smart enough
to turn off.

Thahwasit.


**RACINE**
Damn.
Mama.   Damn.
            We was         we was  w a t c h i n ?

**SHE**
Well
    You   was there.
You was there. He put you down and left.

Them scars you got is from when you tried to get
the fire off me.

**RACINE**
I don't
     rem

          mem

               ber.

**SHE**
Ask your sister if she does.

(*ANAIA is looking away, trying to hide her face.*)

**RACINE**
Twin?
Twin?
You cryin?

**ANAIA**
Umsicktomystomach.
Um sick.

(*ANAIA tries to run away.*)

**RACINE**
Twin? Damn. All emotional.

**SHE**
Where you goin?

(*ANAIA stops in her tracks.*)

Ya can't outrun it
Girl.
Iss gonna meet you wherever you go.

**ANAIA**

I
thought  I thought
                   you was dancin
                              wigglin on the ground like that i thought it was
a dance or somethin. I see it all the time I see it I see you dancin on the ground
with the fire on you like a dress

**SHE**

Shh. Quit cryin, Baby. No need to cry.

**RACINE**

She's sorry, Mama. She just...you know.

**SHE**

Iss somethin I need y'all to do but I don't think
y'all gon be able to do it if she's steady cryin.

**RACINE**

We can do it. We can. We're strong. Ain't we
strong, 'Naia?

**ANAIA**

Yeah.

**RACINE**

We're strong. We can do anything.

**SHE**

Good.
Ima keep this real simple:
Make your daddy dead
                    dead
                    dead
And everything around him you can destroy, too
                    I think he got some  b i t c h

*Is God Is*

## Kill his spirit, then the body
like he did me

## Make him dead real dead
And bring me back some treasures from it.
Gotta do it quick, too. My body ready to go.
We on a time crunch.

### All the way **dead**.

(*A silence.*)

**RACINE**
Uh                     uh                     uh
   uh uh
                  uh                 uh uh
         uhhhh

**RACINE & ANAIA**
Uh    uh                          uhhhh
  **uh** uh                 **uh**
uh                 uh                          uh
         uh   uh

**RACINE**
Mama
we respect that you dyin and all, but uhh
                  this seems a little        crazy—

**SHE**
Not as crazy as settin a woman on fire in front of
her own kids, then abandoning them to go off and
start another life like nothin ever happened.

**RACINE**

...

Okay. You got a point. But uh    uhmm
don't you think that since you dyin you might
wanna just

      forgive and forget? Die in a peaceful state?

**SHE**

Peace will come when he go.

**RACINE**

But Mama—

**SHE**

When he go

**ANAIA**

We ain't killers—

**SHE**

Anaia, pull this sheet offa me.

(*ANAIA does so. A moment during which the TWINS
are aghast. Their mother's body is a hideous thing on
the sheets.*)

No peace 'til I know he gone.
You gonna do this for your mother? This one thing
'fore I die?

**RACINE**

We'll do it.

**SHE**

Good, good. Good girls. Dead. Real dead.

    And bring me back a piece.

**ANAIA**
I don't think—

**RACINE**
Just tell us how to find him.

**SHE**
I don't know where he at but The Lawyer is
out in Californ-eye-ayy near the City of Angels.
Chuck Hall—I'll never forget the name.
Chuck. Hall. He in the Valley. He gon know
where your Daddy's at. Go find him and make
him tell you.

He a slippery motherfucker, so be careful.

# Dead, real dead. Lotsa blood is fine.

\* \* \*

# Going West

*(The Twins are traveling west throughout the following.)*

**RACINE**
Hey Twin.

**ANAIA**
Yeah.

**RACINE**
You ain't sick to your stomach no more?

**ANAIA**
No.

**RACINE**
Good. Well.     She is our mama.

**ANAIA**
But she ain't never came for us, never asked for us—

**RACINE**
I'm sure she kept track of where we was at—

**ANAIA**
It ain't the same.

**RACINE**
How was she gon come see us lookin like that?

**ANAIA**
Like what?

*Is God Is*

**RACINE**
**Like scary.** You know good and well you
woulda shit yourself when you was twelve if
she'da come see you lookin like that talkin 'bout
**"I'm your long lost Mama."**

**ANAIA**
I guess you right.

**RACINE**
Iss just one thing she want us to do before
she die.

**ANAIA**
Yeah. But we ain't killers.

**RACINE**
I am.

**ANAIA**
No, you ain't. Who you done killed?

**RACINE**
Don't worry 'bout all that.

**ANAIA**
Damn, Cine. I mean. She our mama.

**RACINE**
Right.

**ANAIA**
And she made us, so she kinda like God,
like you said—

**RACINE**
Eyup, eyup—

**ANAIA**
And he ain't even like us

**RACINE**
Nope. So. So you ready?

**ANAIA**
...Eyup.

**RACINE**
Good. We gon do this. We gon do it right.

(*They travel in silence for a bit.*)

**ANAIA**
I favor her.

**RACINE**
Who. God?

**ANAIA**
Eyup. The scars I got on my face
she got on her whole self.

**RACINE**
Yeah.

**ANAIA**
I'm glad I favor somebody.

**RACINE**
Yeah. It do look like she spit you out.
Wonder who spit me out.

**ANAIA**
You prolly a combo between both of 'em.

**RACINE**
I 'on know. Whatchoo think he look like?

**ANAIA**
Like a skunk or a snake.
Or a giant with a smelly beard.
He prolly got a beer belly.

**RACINE**
How we gonna kill him?

**ANAIA**
I don't know.

**RACINE**
A gun?

**ANAIA**
Where we gon get a gun?

**RACINE**
Steal one or something.

**ANAIA**
That ain't no good plan.
We should just poison him.

**RACINE**
With what?

**ANAIA**
Strychnine. Arsenic.

**RACINE**
That seem old-fashioned.

**ANAIA**
At least he'll be dead and we ain't gotta really get
no blood on us. I don't like blood.

**RACINE**
But God said lotsa blood is okay.

**ANAIA**
Still.

**RACINE**
Poison
is a punk ass bitch ass way to kill somebody.
    I think we should take a hammer to him.

**ANAIA**
You sick.

**RACINE**
I could do it. Be just like bustin open an egg.

**ANAIA**
Nasty.

**RACINE**
Or stab him?

**ANAIA**
Eugh.
The sound of his body gettin stabbed like meat.
Ima be sick.

**RACINE**
I know! We'll push him off a building.

**ANAIA**
What building?

**RACINE**
We'll find one. We'll get him there close to the
edge and push him.

**ANAIA**
What if he grab one of us on the way down?

**RACINE**
What if we knock him out
      then throw him off the building?

**ANAIA**
How hard do you have to hit someone to knock
them out? I don't like it.

**RACINE**
You don't like any of it.

**ANAIA**
I 'on know
I 'on know about this, 'Cine.
We ain't killers—

**RACINE**
How you figure that? We come from a man who
tried to kill our mama and a mama who wants to
kill that man. Iss in the blood.

**ANAIA**
Ima be sick.        I bet he just look like an
ordinary man.
I used to dream about a lady in a fire
        and I didn't know why.

\* \* \*

# The Weapon

(*The outskirts of the City of Angels. RACINE picks up a sizable rock.*)

**RACINE**
Take your sock off.

(*ANAIA does so. RACINE places the rock in the sock and ties a knot. Ha.*)

**ANAIA**
That for what I think iss for?

**RACINE**
Eyup. Feels right. Like Cain and Abel
or something.

**ANAIA**
She gon get her blood, I guess.

(*They walk on.*)

\* \* \*

# *In The Valley*

(*The Twins stand before the door of a law office in The Valley.*)

**RACINE**
Just follow my lead.

(*RACINE knocks on the door. We're very suddenly inside of the office. HALL sits at a desk.*)

**HALL**
A Mister Chuck Wendell Hall sits at an immense
desk in a North Hollywood office building.
The desk was his grandfather's.
Pure oak very recently refurbished.
The kind of desk that makes a statement.
He sits behind the heavy desk, sweating.
It is the dead of summer. Sweating rivers and rivers.
He wears a shirt with a collar. Expensive. And a necktie,
loosened. Also expensive. If one were to look
below the desk, one would see that he's wearing
Bermuda shorts—not terribly expensive. Orange-ish.
No shoes or socks on his feet.

Dead of summer.

He belches. There is tequila warming
in a glass somewhere nearby.
A fat black fly perched on the edge of the glass
contemplates a swim. His hand shaking, he takes
a bottle of pills from his Bermuda shorts pocket
and attempts to unscrew the cap. Nothing. Child lock.
Fuck.

He tries again, pressing down. The cap opens
and he pours the entire contents of the bottle
onto the desk:

One, two, three...
placing the pills side by side—a pill parade:

four, five, six, seven...
He reaches for the glass of tequila and the fly
buzzes angrily away. Gulp. It barely burns he's
been drinking for hours.

eight, nine, tennn, eleven, twelf, thirteeeen...
He talks to the pills:

I'm going to follow you all straight
                    home
I'm going to follow you
            home, take me there
fourteen, f i f t ee n, s e v e n   t ee n

it is hard to count, three hours he's been drinking

e i g h t ee  n
                    n i n e t ee  n

Okay, okay. Here we go!

And he swallows one—

(*A knock at the door.*)

I'm not here I'm out to lunch I'm retired go away.

(*Another knock.*)

I'm gone! Another pill.

(*A loud bang. He goes to the door and opens it.
THE TWINS are standing there.*)

*Is God Is*

Who

    the

        eff                          you?

            are

**RACINE**
Are you Mr. Hall?

**HALL**
I'm not

        here.

(*Trying to slam the door in their faces, he stumbles and falls to the ground.*)

Oh. Shit.

**ANAIA**
He's drunk.

**RACINE**
Are you Hall?

**HALL**
Why should I tell you anything? I work for-hiccup—
my own self!

**ANAIA**
I think this is him.

**RACINE**
That's his name on the door.

**ANAIA**
But he's drunk as a skunk.

**RACINE**
What that mean?

**ANAIA**

We can't
if he's drunk we can't do it!

**RACINE**

Can't do what?

**ANAIA**

Rough him up or anything. It wouldn't be nice!

**HALL**

You're not the boss of me I'm the boss of myself!

**RACINE**

Shut up!

**HALL**

Don't you tell me to shut up! This is my place.
I built it from the ground up.
You can't just come into a person's place and tell them what to do.

**RACINE**

Definitely him.

**HALL**

Gaddamn right.

**RACINE**

Sit down.

**HALL**

I will. But not because you told me to. I'm sitting down because it's what I wanna do.

*Is God Is*

**RACINE**
Sure.

**ANAIA**
Stinks in here.

**HALL**
That's 'cause Luna's been shitting everywhere
with no regard for anyone but herself.

**RACINE**
Who's Luna?

**HALL**
My receptionist.          Just kidding. The cat.
It was my receptionist's cat but she left it behind
when she left me. Ha haha but your face, though.
You thought it was a human I was talkin about.
Can you imagine some lady squatting
in the corner to drop a deuce? Ha haHa

**ANAIA**
You're disgusting.

**HALL**
I know that you think I don't know that.
It's what she said all the time before she left.

(*Imitating a female voice*)

"Why don't you shave the back of your
neck? You feel like a woolly mammoth.
It's disgusting"

With so much hate. She said it with so much Like she
couldn't stand the very ground I was walking on
How'd that happen We had been in love it had been
love I tell you the first time I saw her—

**RACINE**
Shut up!

**ANAIA**
Don't.

**RACINE**
We need to ask you some things, Mr. Hall.

**HALL**
Do I know you?

**RACINE**            **ANAIA**
Yes.                 No.

**RACINE**
We might know some people in common.

**HALL**
Like who?

**RACINE**
A man from a long time ago. Tried to kill his wife.
Ring a bell?

**HALL**
Lotta bells in the world Church bells, wedding
bells We didn't get married in a church We went
right on down to the courthouse and got it done
She wore a yellow sundress with—

**RACINE**
Sir, we need you to focus.

**ANAIA**
Yes. Please focus.

**HALL**
I am focused. I'm focused. Hell, I won Most
Focused once. Irving Middle School Choir—

**RACINE**
O, my god—

**HALL**
I did! Don't talk to me about focus.

**ANAIA**
Alright, fine. Sir, we really need to find him soon.
We on a time crunch. A man who tried to kill his
wife eighteen years ago. He was a client of yours.
Think about it.

**HALL**
Thinking, thinking.
Mmmmmmnope. Nothing. Don't know who that is.

**RACINE**
You're lyin.

**HALL**
Imagine that.

(*RACINE raises the rock/sock.*)

**HALL**
What's that for?

(*She holds it up higher.*)

**ANAIA**
'Cine.

**RACINE**
I'm gonna have to pop your fat head if you
don't quit playin.

**HALL**
With that?

**RACINE**
What else?

(*HALL is laughing really hard.*)

**HALL**
Is that a rock in there?
    You're gonna hit me to death with
                                    a sock?

(*RACINE swings the rock. He dodges.*)

**ANAIA**
'Cine! Don't—

**HALL**
Missed me!

(*RACINE swings again, again HALL dodges.*)

**ANAIA**
Just give him a chance to tell us—

(*RACINE swings and HALL dodges. He laughs to beat
the band.*)

**HALL**
Okay. No. But seriously. I'm already on my way
out. You almost missed me.

## L o o k i t  here.

*(Holds up the pill bottle and laughs some more.)*

**ANAIA**
What's that?

**HALL**
Pills!
to dispatch myselfffff
Soft and hard and soft
I t o o k 'em I t o o k 'em I t o o k 'em
So Glory is coming! You're too late!
I am bathed in Glory—

**RACINE**
What's he talking about?

**HALL**
You see these shorts? Glory.
Got them in Bermuda.
Lotsa people have Bermuda shorts they
didn't actually get in Bermuda—

**ANAIA**
I think he's sayin he done already took some pills
to kill himself so he don't care about that rock.

**HALL**
That is precisely what he's saying. I've
already taken a few of these. One is enough
to do the magic. Two is enough to have me
dance my way to hell. What do you think
I'll get for a few? I dunno, is it five by now?

*(HALL swallows a few more pills. RACINE lowers
the rock.)*

**ANAIA**
He ain't gonna tell us nothin. He ain't scared to
die. Guess we gotta go.

**RACINE**
We ain't done with this fool.
We gotta find out where—

**ANAIA**
C'mon, 'Cine..

**RACINE**
We got to!

**ANAIA**
Let's just look around. He's got files and things—

**RACINE**
It'll take forever to go through all these
files! God's finna die!

(*Notices that HALL is nodding off.*)

Shit. He's falling asleep—
Hey.   Hey.   You can't fall asleep yet.

**HALL**
Why

                         not?

(*Nodding off*)


**ANAIA**
Please stay awake! God's finna die and we gotta
find out where he at so we can go see him before
She do.

**HALL**
The man you're looking for is your dad.

**ANAIA**
Sort of. He fathered us.

**HALL**
Tall man. Dark man. Lit a lady on fire about
twenty years ago

**RACINE**
Yeah, that's the one!

**HALL**
He lied about it real g o o d
could
     tell he was lying
         but I honestly
             wassso scared of him,
                I just pretended.

**RACINE**
What happened?

**HALL**
In court he said she lit herself on fire
    and we presented old suicide notes she wrote
    when they broke up
    Bastard had them in his pocket when he came
    to see me, before they could even arrest him.
    R e a l  c a l m  and  c o o l .
    Knew he would get off.

**RACINE**
Where he go after y'all won the court case?

**HALL**
Up into the hills.

**ANAIA**
Beverly Hills?

**HALL**
Castaic. Just up the 5.
Little yellow house on the highest hill.
Teal shutters.
Went there for dinner once.
Didn't want to. But.
Neat house. Dog and everything. You'd
never know.

**RACINE**
He livin in a yellow house?

**ANAIA**
With a dog?

**HALL**
Last
I    saw

                       him.

**ANAIA**
What he look like?

**HALL**
Like    like
  he ate
    all
the
     canaries                          and...

(*HALL falls asleep. ANAIA shakes him.*)

**ANAIA**
Mister? Mister?

(*HALL is very suddenly awake again.*)

**HALL**
And he must have a special kind of jizz
'cause he had more
two others     boys
              twinzzzz

**ANAIA**
Twins?

         He got another set of twins?

**HALL**
All the c a n a r i e s.


(*And he succumbs to the pills. They stare at his body a moment.*)


**RACINE**
God said to bring treasure. Iss treasure here.

(*She raises the rock and hits the body. ANAIA runs away. The lights dim. Sound of rock hitting flesh and ANAIA retching.*)


    * * *

# Up to the Hills

(*RACINE and ANAIA are climbing a steep hill.*)

**RACINE**
Twin?
Why you slowin down?

**ANAIA**
Just got a buzzin in my side.

**RACINE**
You wanna take a rest?
We shouldn't be walking all this way, anyhow.
Iss far. Maybe we can thumb a ride or somethin.

(*ANAIA sits in the dust.*)

Sun's going down. We can just sleep out here.
It'll be like camping.

**ANAIA**
'Cept we finna go kill somebody.

(*ANAIA sings softly to herself.*)

**RACINE**
We been killt.

**ANAIA**
Whatchoo mean? We breathin.

**RACINE**
But what we breathin if it ain't been nobody
around to tell us we got mouths and lungs

*Is God Is*

and that make us people like everybody else,
you know?

**ANAIA**
Naw, I don't.

**RACINE**
I mean we floatin
We land from time to time and get stepped
on but thas it.
Ain't been nobody around to give us some
        I don't know
        some foundation?
No real mama. No real daddy. Nobody.

**ANAIA**
You so mad.

**RACINE**
Ain't you? I wanna step on somethin for
once. See what it feel like.        Must feel good.
You 'member Second Foster Daddy?

**ANAIA**
Mmm hmm. With his fat ass.

**RACINE**
'Member how he used to snap the belt at us?

**ANAIA**
Wasn't no "us", that was you. 'Cause you laughed
every time he came down the stairs, so you
always got a whuppin.

**RACINE**
Eyup, eyup.

**ANAIA**
And you used to call for Her. For God. I'd hear you callin for Her from the next room when he was hitting you—

**RACINE**
For Mama?

**ANAIA**
Eyup. You'd be cryin out for Her.

**RACINE**
Thas a lie.

**ANAIA**
No it ain't. I heard you. Ear against the wall—

**RACINE**
You ain't heard me cry. I never cried one time when he was hittin me. Thas why he wouldn't stop. Fat motherfucking fat bitch ass motherfucker. He the first person I killt.

**ANAIA**
You ain't killed him. He had a heart attack.

**RACINE**
He had it 'cause he kept whuppin me. He kept whuppin me 'cause I kept doin stuff to make him whup me 'cause I knew it would kill his fat ass. Fat fuckin ass.

**ANAIA**
Damn.

**RACINE**
Yeah.

*Is God Is*

**ANAIA**
Twin?

**RACINE**
Yeah?

**ANAIA**
Damn.

**RACINE**
I know.

**ANAIA**
You in a room gettin whupped, God layin up with
alligator skin, we got these scars
and he in a yellow house
with teal shutters
and a dog and twins?

**RACINE**
Eyup.

**ANAIA**
New pair. Fresh pair uh twins.

**RACINE**
Don't I know it.
I know it. I know.

**ANAIA**
I like my ugly.

**RACINE**
You ain't ugly.

**ANAIA**
I am and I like it.

**RACINE**

      Stop that.

**ANAIA**

For real. It keeps me safe. Ain't gotta talk to as
many stupid people. They just stay outta my way.
Don't nobody ever hand me no flyer on a street
corner. Iss like a super power.
Damn. I'm burnin.

**RACINE**

Me, too. Scar be burnin like iss still some fire in
there tryna come out.
You ever wanna scrape your scars off and see
what's underneath?

**ANAIA**

Wouldn't nothin be underneath but dead.

**RACINE**

Might be somethin else under there.
I dunno. You might look. Different.
You ever wonder?

**ANAIA**

No point. What we gonna do about them other
twins, Twin?

**RACINE**

God said to destroy everything around him—

**ANAIA**

         could.         could
She said we     She said we    destroy
everything around him.

**RACINE**
Well.

**ANAIA**
"Well" what?
They innocent. They can't help bein his kids.

**RACINE**
Ain't nobody innocent.
They prolly sit up at dinner and laugh about us and God.

**ANAIA**
No, they don't, 'Cine. Stop that.

**RACINE**
Sheeid.

**ANAIA**
They ain't done nothin' to us. C'mon now.

**RACINE**
Fine. Fine. Fine.

(*ANAIA sings a bit to herself.*)

**ANAIA**
Wish it was some ice out here, Twin.

**RACINE**
Me, too.

\* \* \*

# The House on the Hill

(*A modest house in the sleepy desert city of Castaic,
CA. Sound of the family dog barking. RILEY,
SCOTCH and ANGIE are home.*)

**RILEY**
The eldest brother by two minutes, Riley, is
watering the succulents on the balcony.

**SCOTCH**
The younger brother, Scotch, yes, after the liquor,
is in his bedroom writing the best fucking poetry
you've ever heard. If anyone asks, he'll say it's for
school but really it's for him. Them words.

**ANGIE**
Their mother, Angela, is in the driveway unload-
ing the car of a week's worth of groceries.
You boys eat like freaking cows! The least you
could do is come and help me unload.

**RILEY**
Coming.

**SCOTCH**
Coming.

**ANGIE**
Neither is actually coming. Angie stands in the
driveway, the trunk of her car open.
Two cartons of eggs, blueberries, frozen waffles—
mostly for them.

Sweat on her neck she will NOT be carrying
these bags in herself
It's bad enough she had to go to the store and
make sure make sure make sure she got the right
brand of bacon and the correct level of milk fat
It's bad enough the clerk wouldn't accept the
coupon for the peanut butter.
Expired. Expired? Expired.
It's bad enough she stepped in gum and it won't
come off the bottom of her shoe no matter what
she does it won't come off—come off! It won't
Come and get these bags I won't bring them in.
She won't, either. They can sit in this driveway
and melt and churn and spoil
She won't do it
I'll leave them here!
She will too but not really. She'd hate for all of
this stuff to go to waste and the time it took to get
them and anyway, she'd end up looking crazy to
the neighbors who were probably already looking,
peeking up the hill at the house
The top of this hill feels like being in a fishbowl
Not a great neighborhood for being black in
Riley? Scotch?

**RILEY & SCOTCH**
Coming.

**RILEY**
Riley's all about the succulents. They don't really
need much water but it's an excuse.
She's embarrassing, down there yelling and
dowdy with all of her groceries.
So effing house-wife-y, it's embarrassing. So why
not water the succulents or pretend to? Hey, Bruh.
You should go help Mom.

**SCOTCH**
Scotch's poetry is so dope that he refuses to
stop writing.
I mean, the piece uses barbeque as a metaphor for love.
Barbeque as a metaphor for love—chyeah!
Brilliance      I can't, Bruh. I'm writing!

**RILEY**
He can't effng write.

**ANGIE**
Her bunion hurts. She has a bunion. God.

**RILEY**
His metaphors are always clunky.

**ANGIE**
There are black birds circling above. Maybe they
know about the bunion.
Dead of summer.

**RILEY**
Mom, Scotch is gonna come help you.

**SCOTCH**
Scotch recites:
"And Girl, if the sauce gets too dry
on our road to love, Girl
If the sauce gets too dry
from the length of time spent
on the hot coals of life…"
                    This shit so dope!

**ANGIE**
Angie hates her life.

The man occasionally walks into a room and gives
her a look like He wishes she'd disappear already.

The kids won't let her touch them.
And the bunion. Frig. She can't cuss. Hasn't had a
good cuss since the kids.
Your father will be home soon and when He sees
these groceries out here He's going to be very angry!
…

**RILEY & SCOTCH & ANGIE**
Who's she kidding?

**ANGIE**
Tired and pissed does not equal fool. She will put
the groceries away.
The man is not the sort…
She will put the groceries away. Frig.

**RILEY**
Go help Mom.

**SCOTCH**
Shit so dope!

**RILEY**
Dang.

(*He looks over the railing of the balcony.*)

Her mom jeans are extra mom-y today. Sucks teeth.
                                    I got it, Mom. I got it.

**RACINE**
A few yards away hiding behind a neighbor's
minivan.

**ANAIA**
She's pretty.

**RACINE**
So?

**ANAIA**
Just sayin she's pretty.

**RACINE**
Don't.

**RILEY** (*carrying groceries*)
You got everything, huh?

**ANGIE**
What took you so long to come help me?

**RILEY**
Sorry. Was watering the plants.

(*RILEY and ANGIE make their way inside.*)

**ANGIE**
Has your father called?

**RILEY**
Nope.

**ANGIE**
Probably working late tonight.

**SCOTCH**
What's for dinner?

**ANGIE**
You can eat anything you helped me carry inside.

**SCOTCH**
Aw, man, Mom, don't be mad. I'm writing.

**ANGIE**
Angie refuses to be another tired, middle-aged
woman. She refuses. Going out tonight.

**SCOTCH**
Yeah. Clayton and I were thinking of hitting
up a spot—

**ANGIE**
No. I'm going out tonight. Me.

**RILEY**
You?

(*The twins look at their mother.*)

**SCOTCH**
With Dad?

**ANGIE**
With Mrs. Orson.

**SCOTCH**
What, y'all goin to a tea party or something?
Ha haha

**ANGIE**
That's really funny. No. It's a party. Just a regular one.

**SCOTCH**
You gonna make dinner before you go?

**RILEY**
Don't listen to him, Mom.

**ANGIE**
I'm not.

(*ANGIE goes upstairs.*)

**RILEY**
Such a spoiled brat.

**SCOTCH**
What? Y'all need to stop oppressing me for being
so committed to my writing process. I'm trying to
make us all rich.

**RILEY**
Yeah, yeah.

**SCOTCH**
What are you making for dinner?

**RILEY**
Probably do an arugula salad. It's coniferous.
Detoxifying.

**SCOTCH**
It's almost like you're trying to be the lamest
person you can possibly be.

**ANGIE**
Upstairs in the master bedroom, the eyeliner
pencil is slippery.
It is the dead of summer and the boys don't know
what she's planning.
No one knows, not even Mrs. Orson, about the
suitcase packed in the trunk ready to take her to
Yucca Valley where she'll hide out with a friend
and then take the bus to Vegas where she'll
gamble no less than three hundred of the seven
grand she's been saving before taking the train up
to Connecticut, where a new name and job are
waiting for her.
He doesn't hit, He's never done that.
but

but
That look He gave her when she asked
about what happened with His ex-wife

*Is God Is*

That look was. Hm.

    That look    that look was    that was a  l o o k  that
                                            hmmm

*(RILEY knocks on the door.)*

**RILEY**
Mom?

**ANGIE**
What is it, Riley? I'm getting dressed.

**RILEY**
Do you want some salad for the road? Arugula?

**ANGIE**
Had this come from her body?
No, Son. I'm fine. I'll eat out.

**RILEY**
Okay.

                  Mom?

**ANGIE**
Son?

**RILEY**
    i love you.

**ANGIE**
Had this come from her body?  I know, Son.

*(ANGIE opens the door to the room and touches RILEY's face.)*

I love you, too.

*(ANGIE makes her way down the stairs and out the front door.)*

Tell your father I'll be back later on. Keep the door
closed. We aren't cooling the neighborhood.
Scotch—clean your ears. They're dripping. God.
Don't you feel that?

**SCOTCH**
All of my feeling goes into my work.

**ANGIE**
Take care.

**SCOTCH & RILEY**
Bye, Mom.


(*As soon as she closes the door, SCOTCH turns up the
radio. It is incredibly loud. RILEY puts in headphones
and makes dinner. SCOTCH may thrash to his music.*

*ANGIE steps outside and closes the front door.
She gives the house a good, long look and then the
finger. She gets into the car and drives a bit but
doesn't get very far. The TWINS are sitting in middle
of the road. ANAIA sings softly to herself, looking
away. RACINE stares directly at ANGIE.*)


\* \* \*

# In the Road

**ANGIE**
Hello? Hello? Excuse me?
Uh.   Hi? Can you hear me? Helllllloooooooooo!

**RACINE**
We just gon ask her where he at. Thas it. Thas it,
'Naia. You shakin. Stop.

**ANGIE**
HELLOOOOO

**ANAIA**
Ain't you gonna say somethin?

**RACINE**
She gotta come to us.

**ANGIE**
Girls? Can you move, please? Shoo. Shoo!

**RACINE**
Who this bitch think she shooin?

(*ANGIE takes the keys out of the ignition, climbs
out of the car, walking toward the Twins.*)

**ANGIE**
Excuse me, but I've got to be somewhere
          and are you two okay? Is everything alright?

**RACINE**
We fine.

**ANGIE**
She doesn't look well.

**RACINE**
She's fine. You know us?

**ANGIE**
Know you? Uh. No. Should I?

**RACINE**
We're his first ones.

**ANGIE**
Who?

**ANAIA**
His first kids. We're the ones he had first.

**ANGIE**
O.                                        O.
You're alive?

**RACINE**
Naw, we're zombies.

**ANGIE**
He said
He said
you died in some kind of fire and He didn't have to
pay child support.
Are you here for child support?

(*She takes off her pearl necklace, coming closer.*)

Real. Japanese Akoya.

**RACINE**
Don't nobody want your pearls.

**ANGIE**
Well, this what I've got to offer.

**RACINE**
You got more to offer.

**ANGIE**
I need the car.

**RACINE**
You ain't in no position to be tellin us
what you need.
You know what our mama's been doin while you
been layin up in your big yellow house with them
teal shutters?

**ANAIA**
Our mama been up in a bed wastin away. He
burnt up most of her body. She a crisp.

**RACINE**
Eyup. He tried to kill her.
And us, too. See? Fire bit me on my back and arms
and 'Naia on her face.

**ANGIE**
I'm so sorry. That is unfortunate. But I hope
you understand
                    that that    He lied to me—

**RACINE**
You knew he was lyin.

**ANAIA**
'Cine—

**ANGIE**
I didn't.

**RACINE**
Yeah, you did.

**ANGIE**
I did not.

**RACINE**
'Naia, who this heffa think she foolin?
Can't even lie straight.

**ANAIA**
I don't know, 'Cine. She could be tellin the truth—

**RACINE**
You was sittin up in a yellow house with teal
shutters while Daddy number three was makin
us wash his drawz and make him macaroni
outa box and lickin his lips anytime I came
in the room with my shoulders showin—

**ANAIA**
Let's just let her go—

**RACINE**
You was sittin up in a blood house, a house he got
to put a mask on what he done to us.
You ain't ask no questions?

(*ANGIE tries to walk back to the car but RACINE
blocks her path.*)

**ANGIE**
Please. I've got to get away.

**RACINE**
We couldn't get away. Ain't never worn no pearls.
You, 'Naia?

**ANAIA**
Never even held none.

**RACINE**
I like that car. It's a fair reward for all we been through, I think.

**ANGIE**
It's mine.

**RACINE**
Iss ours. He never gave us nothin.
He gave you a lot. And somma what he gave you shoulda been ours.

**ANGIE**
I'm sorry that He—

**RACINE**
Gimme them keys.

**ANGIE**
No.

**RACINE**
What ? Is you stupid?

(*RACINE tries to grab the keys from ANGIE, but ANGIE resists. They struggle a bit.*)

**RACINE**
Gimme the keys, bitch! Give 'em to me!

**ANGIE**
They're mine!

(*RACINE manages to wrench the keys from ANGIE's hand. She holds them up, gleefully.*)

**RACINE**
Got 'em.

**ANGIE**
They don't belong to you!

**RACINE**
Thas whatchyo mouth say!
Look at her, 'Naia. She ain't used to not getting
what she wants.

**ANGIE**
That's just
That's just mean.

**RACINE**
"That's just
That's just mean." Ha ha ha HA ha!

**ANGIE**
You...you pair of animals. You're going
to come and steal from me because
of something He did?

**ANAIA**
We ain't animals. We on a mission. From God.

**ANGIE**
God?

**RACINE**
God is our mama.

**ANGIE**
O, that's right. Your "mama".

**RACINE**
I don't like the way you sayin "Mama"
like that.

**ANGIE**
Well, I don't like having my property stolen
by a couple of thieves!

**ANAIA**
We ain't thieves.

**ANGIE**
Yes you ARE! I just wanna get away
        I just wanna
        I've earned it
        I planned for months
            IF He comes home
and I tell Him the car's been stolen do
you know do you know what He'll...
goddammit Angie you really thought you'd get away, didn't
you you really thought you really did—

**RACINE**
Our mama ain't never had a shot like the one you
got. Sheeid. You ain't special.

**ANGIE**
...It's not   my fault
your weak, ghetto trashy "mama"
got burned up!
She should've left Him!


**ANAIA & RACINE & ANGIE**

..............................................................................

**ANAIA**
....uh....umm

**RACINE**
uh huh, uh umm

**ANAIA & RACINE**
uh um ummm

**ANAIA**
....Bitch...

**RACINE**
...hold up hold up holdup...this Bitch,

**ANAIA**
"Weak"?
"Ghetto trashy"?

**RACINE**
Bitch, where you get all that from?

**ANAIA**
This bitch done called God "ghetto trashy"!

**ANGIE**
Each of us is responsible for how our lives turn
out! If you were educated, you'd understand that—

*(RACINE hits ANGIE in the face with the sock.)*

**RACINE**
We educated.

**ANGIE**
...you hit me...

**ANAIA**
Twin, don't—

**RACINE**
We educated, **Bitch**! Say it. Say we educated!

**ANGIE**
animal

(*RACINE hits ANGIE again.*)

**ANAIA**
Racine!

**ANGIE**
...ow...h a r d—

(*RACINE hits ANGIE a few times.*
*ANAIA hides her face.*)

**ANGIE**
a  i
        r.

(*ANGIE is dead. ANAIA whimpers.*)

**RACINE**
Twin.

**ANAIA**
Yeah?

**RACINE**
You gonna be sick?

**ANAIA**
I don't  think  so.

**RACINE**
You want them pearls?

**ANAIA**
I 'Cine          she dead?

**RACINE**
You ain't did nothin', so you cool. Iss all on me.
If it come up, we'll just tell the truth.
You want them pearls?

**ANAIA**
God might.

**RACINE**
God don't want nothin but blood.
Let's keep one of her nails. They nice. Manicured.

\* \* \*

*Is God Is*

# Twins & Twins

*(Inside the house. SCOTCH and RILEY seated for
a dinner of arugula, piled impossibly high.*

**SCOTCH**
I hate you. You're the worst person alive.

**RILEY**
There's plenty of other food.

**SCOTCH**
Where do you think she really went?

**RILEY**
Don't know. Mexico?

**SCOTCH**
Dad's gonna find her.

**RILEY**
Yeah.

**SCOTCH**
Wanna hear a poem I wrote for her?

**RILEY**
No. Really, no.

**SCOTCH**
It's short.

**RILEY**
God. Please. No.

**SCOTCH**
It's an acrostic that doesn't announce itself:
Matriarch resistant to the matronly
Otherworldly, kind and compassionate
Thoughtful in times of woe or triumph
Holds heaven and earth in her hallowed hands
Even when nothing is enough,
Ride or die wit' it, never shy wit' it
Mother.

**RILEY**
I'm dead.

**SCOTCH**
Jealous.

(*A knock at the door.*)

**RILEY**
Get it. I ordered pizza.

(*SCOTCH goes to the door and opens it.
ANAIA and RACINE stand before him.*)

**SCOTCH**
I know you?

| **RACINE** | **ANAIA** |
|---|---|
| No. | Kind of. |

**RILEY**
Who is it?

**SCOTCH**
Not pizza. Wait. Wait. Our birthday isn't for a
couple of weeks but...

(*RILEY comes to the door.*)

**RILEY**
I didn't actually order pizza...Who's this?

**RACINE**
I'm Racine.

**ANAIA**
Anaia.

**RILEY, SCOTCH, ANAIA & RACINE**
Twins.
................

**SCOTCH**
O shit.
O shit
O shit!

**RILEY**
What?

**SCOTCH**
Dad did this, I think.

**RACINE**
He definitely did.

**SCOTCH**
Come on in, girls! You can change upstairs.
O shit O shit!

**RILEY**
Wait—what are you doing?

**SCOTCH**
Dad hired them!

**RILEY**
How do we know that?

**SCOTCH**
Look at them, Riley! Twins! Stripper twins!

**RILEY**
They don't look like—

**SCOTCH**
I should call Michael and Tyrell—

**RACINE**
Don't call anyone else. Private show.

**SCOTCH**
Okay. Whatever you say, Cutie. Go on up.
Second door on the left.

(*ANAIA and RACINE head upstairs.*)

**SCOTCH**
Oh my god. Stripper Twins! Dad's a genius!

**RILEY**
This just doesn't seem like something he'd do.
Let me just call him and make sure he really
sent them.

**SCOTCH** (*imitating RILEY*)
"Let me just call him..." Do you wake up in the
morning and stroke your chin thinking of ways
to be the lamest motherfucker ever?
Damn.

**RILEY**
I just—

**SCOTCH**
It's our birthday.

**RILEY**
In two weeks.

**SCOTCH**
He always surprises us. Remember the turtles?

**RILEY**
Yes. In our beds while we slept—

**SCOTCH**
Twin fucking turtles we woke up to on our tenth birthday like it was muhfuckin Christmas!

**RILEY**
They stank.

**SCOTCH**
Muhfuckin Turtle Christmas!

**RILEY**
Kinda creepy if you ask me.

**SCOTCH**
Get excited with me, Bro! Twins! We're about to get a striptease from a pair of TWINS! I gotta go get fresh. I call the pretty one.
Ay ay ay! Twins!

(*SCOTCH turns up the radio.*)

\* \* \*

# Dressing

(*ANAIA and RACINE get dressed in the sexiest clothes they can find in ANGIE's closet.*)

**ANAIA**
I don't like this I don't like this I don't like this

(*RACINE holds ANAIA by her shoulders.*)

**RACINE**
We almost there, 'Naia. People always quit just when they 'bout to reach the finish line. Now's not the time to be gettin all emotional. Come on. We almost there. He'll be home soon.

**ANAIA**
This ain't right.

**RACINE**
I said we're almost t h e r e !
Don't get all weak on me now.

**ANAIA**
Fine, then! Go ahead and do what you wanna do but I don't want no part of it.

(*ANAIA turns to leave.*)

**RACINE**
You don't want no part of it?
            You is part of it!

(*ANAIA continues out the door.*)

You just a lil punk!

**ANAIA**
I ain't no punk! Just ain't all hardened like you!

**RACINE**
"Hardened"? The fuck that mean?

**ANAIA**
Means you ain't got no soul or compassion!

**RACINE**
I got soul and compassion for GOD!
Who's finna die!

**ANAIA**
But you ain't got none for nobody else.

**RACINE**
"But you ain't got none for nobody else."
No, I don't!
And why should I?
Huh? Who you see around this
motherfucker I should be havin soul
and compassion for, huh?

**ANAIA**
Okay, fine, fine, fine. Shit. But you gotta promise
me it ain't no more blood but his.

**RACINE**
I promise.

**ANAIA**
You gotta swear to God.

**RACINE**

Fine. I swear 'fore God and to God and I put that on everything. No more blood but his.

**ANAIA**

If you go back on it, I'm just gon walk away, Twin.
Naw, I'm not gon walk. Ima run.
You on your own.

**RACINE**

Let's just get ready.

**ANAIA**

I will.
Don't see why we gotta tease them like we strippers, tho.
Seem weird. They're our brothers—

**RACINE**

Don't you even say that or it becomes true.
They ain't nothin to us and we ain't nothin to them. We on a mission. From God.

**ANAIA**

Twin?

**RACINE**

Yeah.

**ANAIA**

How you felt about killin that lady?

**RACINE**

Nothin.
Don't look at me like that. I didn't feel nothin.
She wasn't a nice lady. And she kinda stole from us. I don't feel nothin for her. All my feelings is for God.

**ANAIA**
Forreal?

**RACINE**
Eyup. God. In between them sheets with her skin flakin off. God prolly ain't been touched by a man since he did it.

**ANAIA**
Nope.

**RACINE**
And what she say? "Ghetto trashy"?

**ANAIA**
I believe thas what she said.

**RACINE**
Now errbody know talkin shit about God will get you kilt.

**ANAIA**
Eyup.

**RACINE**
Struck down.

**ANAIA**
Right.

**RACINE**
We ain't nothin' but the hand of God doin Her bidding.

**ANAIA**
Right. You right.

\* \* \*

# The Tease

(*ANAIA and RACINE come down the stairs, dressed to strip. The radio plays stripping music. RILEY is nearby, watching but not participating.*)

**SCOTCH**
Alright ladies! Let's see what you got!

(*The women dance. RACINE is much more free with her movement than ANAIA. RACINE gives SCOTCH a full on lap dance.*)

Awww, yeahhh! Yes. Yeah, Girl. Work that ass. Work. Hell yeah!

Riley! Twins, Riley! Twins! Hey you

(*points to ANAIA*)

I want you behind me. Put those titties on my neck.

(*ANAIA goes near to him, awkwardly dancing.*)

Wait, wait, wait. Get behind me. Behind. I want this one in the front.

Riley? You better get in on this, Bro. He did it for both of us.

**RILEY**
I'm alright.

**SCOTCH**
No you're not. You. Go dance with my brother.

(*He's pointing at ANAIA, who looks at RILEY.*)

**RILEY**
No, she doesn't need to do that. That's all you, Scotch.

**SCOTCH**
No, Bruh. That's all *you*. I got the pretty one. That one's yours.

(*ANAIA isn't sure where to go. She and RACINE look at one another. ANAIA exits the house.*)

Where's she goin? This isn't over yet. How long did he pay for? Riley?

**RACINE**
My sister ain't ugly.

**SCOTCH**
No, no. I guess, all god's children are beautiful, or whatever. Sure.

\* \* \*

# *All Fall Down*

(*Outside. RILEY follows ANAIA.*)

**RILEY**
Hey. Sorry I don't. I just don't think.
It's not because of your face or anything. I'm just.
This is more Scotch's thing.
You want some water or something?

**ANAIA**
No.

**RILEY**
Okay. Want a coat? Someone might drive by and.
Never mind. So, how long did he pay for?

**ANAIA**
Who?

**RILEY**
My dad.

**ANAIA**
He didn't.

**RILEY**
He didn't?

**ANAIA**
No.

*Is God Is*

**RILEY**
I knew it. I knew you weren't strippers. You just
don't have the—
Something just didn't add up. So, what are you really?

**ANAIA**
Sick. Ima little sick to my stomach.

**RILEY**
O. Anything I can do for you? You want some-
thing to eat? We've got arugula.

**ANAIA**
Thas alright.

**RILEY**
You sound like you're from somewhere in the south.

**ANAIA**
Eyup.

**RILEY**
My dad is, too.

**ANAIA**
...He ever talk about it?

**RILEY**
Not a lot. When he does it's usually to say some-
thing about how fucked up everyone down there
is. How they enjoy swimming in their own misery.

**ANAIA**
Hm.

**RILEY**
I've never really been to the south. Well, Texas
once. Austin. Band trip.

**ANAIA**
How old are you?

**RILEY**
We'll be seventeen in thirteen days.

**ANAIA**
Oh. Bet you got you a girlfriend.

**RILEY**
No.

**ANAIA**
Cute little kid like you?

**RILEY**
There's
there's this guy I like.

**ANAIA**
Oh. My bad.

**RILEY**
I hope you don't mind my asking......
What happened to your face?

**ANAIA**
Thas a secret.

(*A scream from within the house.*)

**RILEY**
You hear that?

**ANAIA**
Yeah. Seems like they're havin a good time.

(*Another scream.*)

*Is God Is*

**RILEY**
No No
That sounded bad.

**ANAIA**
They're fine. My sister, she just gets a little wild.

**RILEY**
Maybe I should—

**ANAIA**
It was a fire. Someone set a fire and it crawled onto my face and left me like this.

**RILEY**
O, wow. That sucks. Why would anyone do something like that?

**ANAIA**
Thas what I keep askin myself. How could he?

**RILEY**
He? You know who did it?

(*Another scream as SCOTCH runs out of the house.*)

**SCOTCH**

R i l e y!!

The    pretty        tried    to to
      one            to—

(*SCOTCH falls to the ground, crawling. We can see a knife stuck in his back.*)

**RILEY**
Scotch! Scotch! There's a knife in you!


**SCOTCH**
Is       that
            w h a t       t h a t  i $_s$?

*(RILEY tries to pull the knife from his brother's back.)*

No
hurts
no


**RILEY**
O
  my god    O my god
                       what
O my god
    How O my god

*(RACINE appears from inside of the house, less dressed than when we last saw her and bloody. She holds the sock. RILEY tries to stop the blood pouring out of his brother with his hands.)*


**SCOTCH**
I
i i i'm—


**RILEY**
Don't.
**DON'T!**


**SCOTCH**
ahh h ha ha l  a  m  e...

*(SCOTCH is gone.)*

**RILEY**

Ha ha          HA              ha          haHa
ha
                  ha haha                    ha

hahhaha
              HAHA                    Ha hah haha


Scotch is
Scotch is
                  Scotch is my
                              twin  dead!
                  Scotch is my twin is
Ha aha hAHAhaha haha Ha HaaaaaAAA
He's dead   His blood is   He's gone
My twin
Gone
                                    This is  f u nn y y y y


ha ha HAHA ha                    hahA    Ha ha a
h  a  ha h aaaa ha HHhhaa


Ha    ha HAA   HA HA HA ha haha  he's bleeeeding


arugula arugula on his SHIRT ha ha ha!  Ha
And and          and and and he HATES arugula!
Ha ha ha!


**RACINE**
Look like he done went crazy.


**ANAIA**
Yeah. Yeah.


**RACINE**
He called you ugly. I didn't plan to do it, but he
called you ugly.


**ANAIA**
                  I am, though.

**RACINE**
If we don't do the other one, he's gonna tell.

**ANAIA**
What? No.

**RACINE**
You don't have to watch. You can go inside.

**ANAIA**
You said...you said...

**RACINE**
He'll talk. He might even blame you even though you didn't do it—

**ANAIA**
We talked. Me and him.

**RACINE**
What that mean?

**ANAIA**
Means we can't.

(*RACINE goes to approach RILEY but ANAIA stands in her way.*)

**RACINE**
You in my way.

**ANAIA**
You keep doin it. You said we'd just do him and not them but—

**RACINE**
I'm doin what's best for us—

**ANAIA**
You a lie.

**RACINE**
Get the fuck outta my way, Twin—

(*RACINE tries to pass ANAIA, but ANAIA shoves her.*)

G i r r r l

(*ANAIA shoves her sister again.*)

Punk ass.
Punk ass bitch!
Say it. Say "I'm a punk ass weak ass bitch—

**ANAIA**
Stop.

**RACINE**
If you start cryin, I swear to god—

**ANAIA**
Twin—

**RACINE**
You in my way. God gon be mad when I tell Her—

**RILEY**
Why are you doing this?

**ANAIA**
Because your daddy is our daddy and he—

**RACINE**
Don't talk to him!

**RILEY**
My dad is...?

**ANAIA**
Your dad did a bad thing to our mama.

**RACINE**
Jesus Christ.

**RILEY**
O. That sucks.

**RACINE**
Let's do him before he gets away and tells on us—

**RILEY**
Is He the one that burned you?

**ANAIA**
Yes. And I know it's not your fault. Don't worry. We're not going to hurt you.

**RACINE**
This shit right here

(*ANAIA sits beside RILEY.*)

**RILEY**
Thank you.

(*RILEY grabs ANAIA's throat. RACINE hits RILEY with the sock. He collapses.*)

**RACINE**
What I tell you? Huh? You wanna make conversation with him? You so—

(*RILEY has gotten up and tackles RACINE. He bests her and straddles her body, his fingers tight around her neck. ANAIA tries unsuccessfully to get him off of her sister.*)

*Is God Is*

**RILEY**

Crazy crazy bitch! You want to come to my
house and kill my brother **Bitch** I don't care
what He did **Die**! Die, you. Die
There you go. Just go. Die.
Stupid, filthy, disgusting, dog bitch
Die die die Die die—

(*ANAIA has hit RILEY as hard as she can on the back
of his head with the sock. She hits him again and
again until he gurgles, twitches, and is still. ANAIA
goes to RACINE, shaking her.*)

**ANAIA**

O-'Cine-he's-gone-I-I did it-he's—

...

Twin? Twin? 'Cine, get up.

(*Sound of a car approaching. She looks in the
direction it's coming—up the driveway. She shakes
RACINE again.*)

**ANAIA**

Get up. Somebody's comin.

(*The car stops. ANAIA lifts her sister, dragging her
out of view. She waits. A car door opens and closes
and MAN gets out. We hear hard-soled shoes on the
ground. He stops near RILEY's body for a moment.
He continues, stopping at SCOTCH's body. He walks
near the bushes, very close to where ANAIA is hiding,
then turns again towards the car.*

*In the driveway he takes off his shoes and socks,
slowly, methodically. He removes his suit jacket and
tie. He rolls up his pants legs, whistling. Finally, he
takes off his hat and we see his face for the first time.*)

**MAN**

This slope continues right on up just behind the
house. Pretty easy climb if you're in decent shape.
Meet me at the top.

Or. You could just stay in those bushes

and wonder.

*(MAN climbs the aforementioned hill. ANAIA
emerges from the bushes, laying her sister down
on the ground carefully.)*

**ANAIA**

Twin. He's here. I'm gonna...

I got the sock. I got it.

*(She follows MAN up the hill.)*

\* \* \*

*Is God Is*

# *Showdown*

*(ANAIA and MAN stand on opposite sides of the hill.)*

**MAN**
You still kinda pretty. Kinda. You ain't a complete monster. I was worried.

**ANAIA**
Huhwhat?

**MAN**
Well, maybe just plain "pretty" in general is a stretch. You're prettier than I left her, that's for sure. Well. You want to ask me some questions, I imagine.

**ANAIA**
Huhwhat?

**MAN**
How about if I ask one and then you ask one. You first.

**ANAIA**
I    I

I don't know—

**MAN**
Yes, you do.

**ANAIA**
I
Why did you set her on fire?

**MAN**
Because she wouldn't let me hold her.

**ANAIA**
You set—wait, what does that—

**MAN**
My turn. Who'd you kill first?

**ANAIA**
I didn't kill nobody. Not really, 'cept in self defense. 'Cine was the one—

**MAN**
Who first?

**ANAIA**
Your wife.

**MAN**
Angie?

**ANAIA**
Thas her name? Yeah.

**MAN**
Wow.

**ANAIA**
My turn. What does that mean "she wouldn't let me hold her"? Huh? You were mad 'cause she didn't want you to touch her so you set her on fire?

**MAN**
It's more nuanced than that, but yes.

**ANAIA**
That don't strike you as a bit of an overreaction?

**MAN**
My turn. How'd she die?

**ANAIA**
Your wife? Rock in a sock. You don't think you overreacted a lil bit?

**MAN**
It was an appropriate response by a man out of control, I admit. I was young.

**ANAIA**
"Appropriate"? "Appropriate"? You are really sick.

**MAN**
You ever have a blemish you want to get rid of very, very badly?
A blackhead, maybe? You ever squeeze the blackhead until it falls off but there's pus underneath still hanging around? Reminding you of the ugliness of that blackhead?
Then it becomes about getting rid of the puss with peroxide or whatever you can find that'll sting just a little so you know it's working? You ever just need to put a thing out because it has been so catastrophic to your very being?

**ANAIA**
Pus?

**MAN**
I was young.

**ANAIA**
Just something for you to get rid of?

**MAN**

I was young. And I'm sorry. Next thing I did was go down to the bridge over the river and hang over it, ready to jump in so I could join you all in death.

**ANAIA**

But you didn't.

**MAN**

No. And thankfully, you all survived.

**ANAIA**

But you went to court and got off and God is in a bed burnt to a crisp and I'm so ugly no one'll look me in my eyes.

**MAN**

I'm sorry about that. But it isn't just my fault. You've got to factor in every piece of the puzzle.

**ANAIA**

Every    piece  of the
                p u z z l e?
                What other pieces are there?

**MAN**

She could've let me hold her. She could've opened herself up to me. She could've let me fully stand up in my house. I needed that as a young man. Just to fully stand.
I don't expect you to understand.

**ANAIA**

Igotababycomin.
You're the granddad.
A baby.

**MAN**
You're not a killer.

**ANAIA**
What am I gonna tell the baby 'bout all
of this?

**MAN**
Put that thing down. You can tell it you made a
few mistakes when you were young. Like I did.

**ANAIA**
How am I gonna tell it 'bout God and 'Cine
and you?
'Bout how you tried to
                              k  i  l  l    us all.

**MAN**
"Kill us all"?
I didn't try to kill you all. Just her. You think I set
my own babies on fire?
She did that. She screamed and grabbed ahold of
you two.
I couldn't get her to let go. That's when I ran out.
That's why I stood on that bridge and nearly let
myself fall in.
You think I tried to kill my own babies? Is that
what she told you?

**ANAIA**
...

**MAN**
I didn't. She lied.

**ANAIA**
I promised God I'd bring back a piece of you.

**MAN**

I'm telling you, she lied. You've got to give this up.
Otherwise it's just going to be bad for all time.
You'll try to kill me and I'll have no choice but to
kill you
and in doing so I'll be killing my first grandchild.
I don't want to do that.

**ANAIA**

O       my       god       where       am

                                                  I?

**MAN**

Anaia.
You came out so pretty. Be a pretty mother to
your baby.
Come on. Put it down and I'll walk you down
that hill and you'll go tell her whatever you need
to tell her
and when that baby comes you'll bring it back
and I'll bounce it on my knee
and we'll never talk about all the blood on the
ground.
We'll brush it away like a cobweb.
Come on. I've got to bury my dead.
We're the only ones left.

(*ANAIA lowers the sock. He goes to her and takes her
hand gently.*)

How far along are you?

**ANAIA**

Eleven weeks.

(*He slaps her. Hard. She cradles her face, collapsing
to the ground.*)

**MAN**
That older one, the smart one, he was gonna
be **somebody.**

**Dog bitch.**

If you weren't pregnant I'd cut your eyes
out and make you

**eat**
**them.**

*(He kicks her and she tumbles down the hill.)*

Go back to that  h

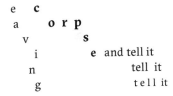 e    **c**

a        **o r p**

v                **s**

i            **e**  and tell it

n                    tell it

g                    t e l l  it

I'd do it  **a l l  agai**n  if  i  could

*(ANAIA struggles to stand. MAN places the bodies
of his sons near to one another. He takes a flask from
his coat pocket and pours it on them.*

*ANAIA has gotten to her feet. MAN eyeballs her.)*

**ANAIA**
While you was here whistling and making new babies and
trying to forget all the bad things you did,
Fourth Foster Mama was laughin at my scars with her friends.

**MAN**
I warned you.

**ANAIA**
Either you or me or somebody got to go today. World can't hold us both.

**MAN**
Suit yourself.

(*He moves toward her but RACINE jumps on his back.*)

**ANAIA**
'Cine!

**MAN**
Get off me!

(*MAN is swinging around, trying to get RACINE off.*)

**RACINE**
K i l l  him, 'Naia!

(*ANAIA hits MAN in the belly with the rock as hard as she can. He keels over. The Twins descend on his fallen frame, kicking and stomping him. RACINE takes the rock from her sister and brings it down on him repeatedly.*)

**RACINE**
You
ain't
n o t h i n,
       **now**

**ANAIA**
Yeah
Yeah
N o t h i n

*Is God Is*

### RACINE

J
 u
  s
   t
      a  s o f t
       s p o t  on the
                      n  d
                   o  u
                 r
               g
       Y o u
       can't hit n o b o d y can't H I T no body no more
       can't set nobody on f i r e can't marry some p r i ssy biiiitch
       can't go have no new b a b i e s can't hurt God you n o t h in

### ANAIA & RACINE
can't do n o b o d y like that you ain't N O T H I N y o u the one thas wrong
crawl you down there grind crawl N O T H I N monster ugly belly giant snake
you the one ain't 'bout shit N O T H I N you the one that got left you you
what you gonna do now ain't N O T H I N got no mama, no daddy no
place to put your feet up  N O T H I N you gon stay downyou

(*RACINE takes the liquor and pours it all over MAN's
battered face. She takes his matches from the ground
and strikes one.*)

### MAN
W a i t w a i t w a i t

### RACINE
He
u l
  g y,
ain't he, Twin?

### ANAIA
Eyup.

(*RACINE drops the match, setting MAN ablaze.
He burns, writhes and screams.*)

Let's go.

(*The pair turn to leave, but MAN grabs RACINE's foot. The flame quickly travels up her leg.*)

**RACINE**
Get off me,
**mother
     fucker!**
Get off!
     Let go!

**ANAIA**
'Cine?

(*RACINE cannot shake him off, though she fights hard. He pulls her closer. The flame engulfs her. She falls to the ground.*)

**RACINE**

'Naia help get him off me 'Naia!

(*ANAIA takes a few steps back.*)

'N a i a

(*ANAIA takes a few more steps back.*)

**ANAIA**
i
i can't, Twin

**RACINE**
Get burnin Get Twin burnin
  him Twin him isss isss
burnin issississ b u r n inn iss s ss ssss burnin iss ss
sss ssss s ss s s s s s ssss ssss s s s s s s ss s s s s s s s s ssssss s s s

*Is God Is*

**ANAIA**

t'naC

**RACINE**
Twin?  T w i n?  T
                        w      n ?
                    t w   i n ?
                        w      n
                    t              ?


(*ANAIA runs and hides as her sister screams.
The fire burns until everything is ash.*)


\* \* \*

# *Twin?*

(*ANAIA makes her way from her hiding place.*)

**ANAIA**
Them b u r n i n
Them b u r n i n twi—
Anaia is too tired for this too tired she's too tired
she's too tired for this
for this                                    Twin
For this she's too tired
'Naia lookin out like somebody could see her
without  f l i n c h i n g
                    she  l o o k i n   o u t

(*ANAIA looks out at us.*)

**ANAIA**
She lower her head out of habit.

(*She leaves.*)

\* \* \*

# Again Before God

(*ANAIA stands before her mother, whose breath is coming in loose gasps. She is dwindling.*)

**SHE**
Well?

**ANAIA**
He's gone.

**SHE**
And your sister?

**ANAIA**
Her too.

(*ANAIA places the pieces of each of those killed before SHE—an ear, a manicured nail, MAN's hat, etc.*)

**SHE**
One, two, three, four, five.
Well, well. You did it.
I ain't tryna be funny, but I didn't think you'd be the one.

**ANAIA**
Yeah.

**SHE**
Reason you got burnt up worst is you was the one tryin hardest to save me.
Guess that shoulda tol me something 'bout how dedicated you are.

**ANAIA**
Yeah

**SHE**
You alright, Baby?

**ANAIA**
'Cine
'Cine died

          and
          and
            you ain't even you ain't e'en

she dead, Mama. Dead.

He said....he told me you was the one...

**SHE**
What's that?

**ANAIA**
I got a baby comin. Ima name it Enica  Thas almost
Racine spelled backwards.
Whatchoo think?

**SHE**
Clever.

(*ANAIA raises the sock/rock above her mother's head.
SHE cannot see it.*)

**ANAIA**
Mama
Mama                we cursed? Feel like it.

**SHE**
Hard to say.

**ANAIA**
Mama
You feel like you can die in peace, now?

**SHE**
Eyup. Iss real  q u i e t  now.

**ANAIA**
Funny
I still hear noise.

*(The almost imperceptible sound of a lullaby.*

*ANAIA lowers the rock/sock.*

*End.)*

* * *

**ALESHEA HARRIS'** epic western revenge play *Is God Is* (world premiere directed by Taibi Magar at Soho Rep) won the 2016 Relentless Award, an OBIE award for playwriting, the Helen Merrill Playwriting Award and was a finalist for the Susan Smith Blackburn Prize. *What to Send Up When It Goes Down*, a ritualized response to anti-blackness, had its critically-acclaimed NYC premier (dir. Whitney White, produced by The Movement Theatre Company), then toured D.C. and Boston in fall of 2019, was featured in American Theatre Magazine's April '19 issue and won a rare Special Commendation from the 2020 Blackburn Prize. Harris was awarded the Next Step Award from Samuel French and is a recipient of the 2020 Windham-Campbell Literature Prize.

**3 Hole Press** titles:

IS GOD IS—Aleshea Harris, 2017

BRIEF CHRONICLE, BOOKS 6-8—Agnes Borinsky, 2017

WHEELCHAIR—Will Arbery, 2018

THE IMMEASURABLE WANT OF LIGHT—Daaimah Mubashshir, 2018

BOUQUET—Mariana Valencia, 2019

MORE STUPIDS—Emmy Bright, 2020

COOKING AS THOUGH YOU MIGHT COOK AGAIN—Danny Licht,
    2020 (forthcoming)

For more information about **3 Hole**, visit 3holepress.org

*Is God Is*